BUILDING MISSIONARY CONGREGATIONS

towards a post-modern way of being church

*by Robert Warren: The Church of England's
National Officer for Evangelism*

BOARD OF MISSION OCCASIONAL PAPER NO.4

ISBN 0 7151 5532 6

Published 1995 for the Board of Mission of the General Synod of the Church of England by Church House Publishing

© *The Central Board of Finance of the Church of England*

Fourth impression 1997

Cover design by Julian Smith
Printed in Scotland by Bell and Bain Ltd, Glasgow
Production organised by Indeprint Print Production Services, London

CONTENTS

PREFACE

As Chairman of the Board of Mission I am pleased to commend this paper for consideration and action by the Church. It represents the fruit of the work of Canon Robert Warren during his first year as the Board's National Officer for Evangelism as he has reflected on the Lambeth 88 call for the Church of England to become 'a movement for mission'. Whilst the Board welcomes this paper as a valuable contribution to discussion, the views expressed are not to be understood as necessarily the policy of the Board of Mission.

The paper is not intended to be the last word on the subject. Nor is it a practical 'how to' document. More work needs to be done before such resources will emerge. Rather, it is intended to stimulate thought about how the Church should be the Church as it prepares to enter the third millennium. In view of the rapidly changing culture in which we live, this is an important issue. In this debate both 'revolutionists' and 'evolutionists' will hopefully develop their arguments.

The paper should be understood within the wider context of the Church. 'Missionary congregations' were first written about in the World Council of Churches' booklet *The Church for Others* in 1968. The WCC has continued to explore the subject. In addition, the Council of Churches for Britain and Ireland is developing a long-term process designed to explore this issue which will doubtless, at the ecumenical level, contribute significantly towards any 'movement in mission' of the whole church. The Roman Catholic Church in Ireland, the Church of Scotland and the WCC in Europe, have all been making significant contributions to this subject.

For all these reasons 'missionary congregations' appears to be 'an idea whose time has come'. The Board therefore commends this paper for consideration and action by the Church.

The Rt Revd Dr Thomas Butler
Bishop of Leicester, Chairman of the Board of Mission.

Introduction

It is time to give attention to how the church is the church. Our present way of being church is, after all, profoundly shaped by the establishment of Christendom over fifteen hundred years ago. The church of the catacombs was a very different way of being church from the one we know today. Equally, the Celtic church functioned in a significantly different way from the way that the Roman church, which replaced it, operated. After so long a period, it would seem wise to take the church in for a service. Moreover there are particular reasons for suggesting such an overhaul today.

Little attention has been paid to the church as the primary agent of mission

We have thought of the great *evangelists*, Moody and Finney in the 19th century, and the likes of Billy Graham and David Watson, and of *evangelistic events* and services. We are increasingly aware of the *process* of conversion, and adjusting our evangelistic structures to that insight. We have also thought of the *individual* Christian as evangelist; rightly so, as the research of John Finney in *Finding Faith Today* has so clearly established eighty per cent of those who come to faith attribute friendship with a church member as the single most important factor. But notice that – friendship with a *church member*. It is not just the one-to-one relationship (though it is that), but also the way in which that relationship opens the door into a community living the gospel.

> *The only hermeneutic of the gospel, is a congregation of men and women who believe it and live by it.*
> Lesslie Newbigin, *The Gospel in a Pluralist Society*, p.227

One of the fascinating things about the New Testament epistles is the lack of emphasis on evangelism. Every now and again a phrase or sentence points in that direction, yet it does not seem to be a major thrust. What undoubtedly is central is the outworking of the faith in personal behaviour and in the life of the community of faith. Building the faith community seems to be central to what the writers of the epistles saw as the work of evangelism. This certainly seemed to be how the apostle Paul saw being church as the way of doing mission:

> *The Lord's message rang out from you not only in Macedonia and Achaia – your faith in God has become known everywhere. Therefore we do not need to say anything about it . . . 1 Thessalonians 1:8*

What is all too easily overlooked is that *the church is the primary agent of mission*. How, and how well, the church functions in that role is crucial to the work of evangelism and the subject of this paper.

The state of the church demands attention and action

There is much that is good, and even prophetic, about the life of the church. Hidden works of great generosity, care and service, individuals of great passion and compassion, people in high office affecting the whole tone of society, remarkable stories of conversion and changed lives through personal encounters with God, are all signs of God's kingdom at work in and through the church.

But the other side must be faced. Declining numbers in many churches, falling numbers of ordinands over four decades, costly and inappropriate buildings, the continual threat of lack of resources (people and money) to keep the existing structure going, and the sheer irrelevance of so much church life are marks of today's church which we neglect at our peril.

> *For the majority of people in this country our churches are irrelevant, peripheral and seemingly only concerned with their own trivial pursuits.*
>
> Robin Greenwood, *Reclaiming the Church*, p.156

No commercial operation would have waited as long as the Church of England has done before developing a corporate strategy to deal with the situation. Yes, the church is more than a corporate structure – but it is not less than one. It appears too easily like the Co-op trying to 're-package the divvy', when the whole culture out of which the 'divvy' arose, has moved on to something very different.

After decline in church membership over most of this century, it is late in the day for the church to face this disturbing fact. It was nobly attempted under Archbishop William Temple, in the fine report *Towards the Conversion of England*, but no coherent or deliberate action followed. This is why today, alongside the encouragement of one-to-one faith-sharing and evangelistic activities, the deeper questions need to be addressed about how the church is the church, and whether our present way of being church is the only or best way.

The decade of evangelism deserves a re-working of the nature of the church

It really is important, in this decade, especially in the light of the present state of the church, that we do something more strategic than simply increase the amount of evangelistic activity. Whilst it is important to be *doing* evangelism, it is even more vital that we learn better ways of *being* evangelistic by the way the church operates.

For significant change to be brought about there needs to be a shift in the fundamentals. Indeed if we could achieve such a shift, rather than overburden hard-pressed clergy and congregations with yet one more task (evangelism) on top of an already full agenda, we might well not only forward the mission of the church but at the same time reduce the level of exhaustion in the church and amongst the clergy. That would be good news indeed.

The bishops have told us to reshape the nature of the church

That a great moment of opportunity stands before us is evidenced by the fact of the church's commitment to pursue a decade of evangelism, and by the nature of that commitment, springing as it did from the Lambeth Conference of bishops in 1988. Clearly the commitment then was to something more fundamental than simply increasing the amount of evangelistic activity, important though that is. That Conference expressed itself in these terms:

> *This Conference calls for a shift to a dynamic missionary emphasis going beyond care and nurture to proclamation and service.*
>
> *Recommendation 44, Lambeth Conference 1988*
>
> *In many parts of the world, Anglicans have emphasised the pastoral model of ministry at the expense of mission. We believe that the Holy Spirit is now leading us to become a movement for Mission.*
>
> *Lambeth pastoral letter, 7.13, p.327*

Defining terms

Before proceeding any further it is important to explain the use of the terms 'pastoral' and 'missionary'. They are used for several reasons, not least that these are the words used at Lambeth 88. They need to be understood as terms which define how the church is the church in terms of two contrasting settings of the church. The church in 'pastoral mode' is a church in a Christendom setting where the vast majority of the population are baptised and, notionally at least, Christian. Such a culture can be described as 'Christian' because the values and worldview of that culture stem from Christian roots. The church in 'mission mode' is, in contrast, set in a culture where a number of competing value systems and worldviews exist alongside each other. Such is the present setting of the church.

We are living in a new missionary age in *this* country.
Robin Greenwood, *Reclaiming the Church,* p.47

This is why we need a missionary church.

These terms are also used simply because they are not simple black and white distinctions. There is much that is good about the church in pastoral mode, much that needs to be carried forward into new ways of being church, but it needs to be harnessed to the new missionary setting of the church. There are also dangers facing the church in mission mode, which will be explored later. So the task is not to abandon the old, bad, pastoral mode and adopt the new, good, mission mode. Rather, the argument of this paper is that we need to recognise the downside of the church in pastoral mode within our new missionary setting and taking with us the good things from that mode find new ways of being church.

Another way of expressing this pastoral/mission distinction would be to talk about *inherited* and *emerging* ways of being church. Those who find such terms more helpful simply need to substitute these words whenever the words *pastoral* and *mission* are used.

At the heart of the distinction that is being made in this paper between a pastoral and missionary church, is the difference between a church organised around sustaining, developing and promoting its own life, and a church organised around participating in God's mission in the world to establish his redemptive purposes in the whole of human life. A working definition of a missionary congregation is thus:

> *A missionary congregation is a church which takes its identity, priorities, and agenda, from participation in God's mission in the world.*

There is a further reason for paying attention to how the church is the church and it is of such importance that it needs to be considered in a separate chapter. That reason is that our society is in a period of such profound transition that we need some understanding of the changes taking place if we are ever to develop a way of being church that is appropriate to the changing circumstances which confront us. To these changes in society we now turn.

Chapter 1

Culture shift as the context for mission

If the church is to become a missionary church the first task is to under-stand the culture to which we have been sent. This is how any missionary would proceed. For us the task is somewhat more difficult not as a result of the strangeness of the community to which we are sent, but rather because it is so familiar to us. *Its* culture is *our* culture; which makes it that much more difficult to distinguish between what is 'gospel' and what is 'culture'. This is the challenge which faces the indigenous church in any culture.

Although the modern missionary movement has been instrumental in taking the gospel to the four corners of the world, it is also widely acknowledged now that, in our cultural blindness, we also took more of our own culture, wrapped up in our message, than we should have done. Having learned that lesson on the mission field, we now have to learn it at home. We need to distinguish between what is gospel and what is culture in our own setting. Moreover, we need to learn again the skill of reading culture, as the Celtic missionaries who first brought the gospel to this country did so well. As Bishop Gitari of Kenya put it at the Lambeth Conference of 1988 (see Tom and Barbara Butler's book, *Just Mission*, page 73ff), we need to discern what is good in our culture and can be affirmed, what is neutral and is to be adapted to, and what is wrong and is to be confronted. We also need to identify trends, what is changing, and how we are to respond to them. It is also important for us to reflect on the culture, or style of operating, of the church and ask whether it is the best or most appropriate way of being church in this culture.

There are resources which can come to our aid in this work of under-standing and speaking into our culture. The worldwide church and the missionary organisations of the church have skills which the church in England badly needs. Partners in Mission is a vital reality, not an empty phrase. We would be foolish indeed not to seek the help of others more experienced than we are, in this global village, to help in the missionary endeavour of understanding our culture.

There are also resources nearer at home on which we can draw. The writing of Lesslie Newbigin and the work of the 'Gospel and Our Culture project', and the C.S. Lewis Centre, have already begun the vital ground work. More recently, and from a fresh perspective, is the work of Graham Cray (in his Board of Mission Occasional Paper *From Here to Where?*).

Indeed this booklet is in many ways a development of the perspectives on culture outlined in that Occasional Paper.

For the purposes of this paper, a few headlines will alert us to the context in which the church is called to fulfil its mission. They are as follows:

(a)   *We are living in a period of great upheaval and transition.* Many writers have pointed out the potential instability of modern culture, as well as its being a period of accelerated change. Typical of such perceptions are the following:

> **The situation in the scientific and affluent West is not stable. We cannot assume that our present day spiritually inadequate but materially and politically successful societies will continue.**
> Bryan Appleyard, *Understanding the Present,* p.232.

> **We are living in the greatest revolution in history, a huge, spontaneous upheaval of the entire human race. Not a revolution planned and carried out by any particular party, race or nation, but a deep elemental boiling over of all the inner contradictions that have ever been in people, a revolution of the chaotic forces inside everybody. This is not something we have chosen nor is it anything we are free to avoid.**
> Thomas Merton, *(1950s)*

> **The human race finds itself today in a new period of her history, characterised by profound and accelerated changes which progressively extend to the entire universe.**
> Vatican II, *The Church in the Modern World, No.4*

Our culture is at the end of the shelf-life of a number of its primary shaping characteristics.

(b)   *We are living in the end times of Christendom,* literally 'Christ's-kingdom' in which the church authenticated and defined the nature of secular authority. The background information, worldview and value-system, in such a society, were fundamentally Christian. Society was held together by a common knowledge of biblical images, such as God as creator, the Good Samaritan, and by a common value system in which the ten commandments were accepted as the only framework within which the laws of society could be shaped.

6

Now the old order is changing. We inhabit a multi-faith, multi-cultural society. Evangelism can no longer be a matter of taking out the message to a world which accepts the fundamentals. It will involve the missionary endeavour of translating the gospel into other cultures, and learning to speak new cultural languages. Mission can no longer proceed on the basis of asserting external authority. The church must recover the servant nature of the missionary endeavour if it is to communicate in the contemporary setting.

(c) *We are living in the end times also of the Enlightenment culture* in which reason reigned as king. It has produced a remarkable technological, as well as a bureaucratic, culture. It has proceeded by analysis, taking life apart, and seeking to understand the whole by means of a detailed analysis of the parts. It has looked at all of life, creation and humanity included, and sought to understand them as a mechanism. Such a view is breaking down. Creation, society and the individual are being found to be more alive than that. So today's thinking looks much more in the direction of seeing that the whole is greater than the sum of the parts. The emerging culture is marked by the holistic, rather than analytical, approach. Certainly the Christian will assert the value of reason as a God-given gift, but we will want to restore it to its integrated place in life, rather than from the detached analytical place to which it has often been reduced.

(d) *We are also living at the end of the Age of Modernism,* the longing for the new and the abandoning not only of all that was associated with the past but also, in existentialist fervour, an abandoning of any perception of there being a future. From such a perspective 'now' is the only time. The Christian faith, whilst affirming the importance of living in the present moment, points also to a present rooted in the past and on route to a future.

For these reasons the word most frequently used to describe our culture is the word 'post-', as in post-Christian, post-Enlightenment and, more particularly, *post*-modern. The use of that prefix (*post-*) needs to be clarified.

It does not mean the abandoning of that which is past. Hopefully we take with us many discoveries and developments which have enhanced life in society. A post-Christendom culture is not the same as a pre-Christian culture, we take our experience with us. However, 'post-' alerts us to the fact that we are moving into something different. What it does not tell us is what that 'something else' is. 'Post-' is something of an interim term suggestive of a *transition*, even if we do not yet know what to. Most adults today are likely to spend all their days in that transition period. We will need to be bi-lingual; able to relate to those who belong to the old order, as well as to those who live in the new.

7

It should be added here that the three 'end time' elements identified above are a considerable simplification of a very complex situation. Some major cross-currents point to the fact that the period of transition in which we live is not a simple one-way system or predictable motorway. The restructuring of the National Health Service around the internal market is just one example of the way in which viewing reality as a machine and system is growing and gaining ground at the same time that the philosophical basis of such an approach is being brought into question. This is what makes predicting the shape of things to come such an uncertain science.

However, what many commentators, from different faiths and from no faith backgrounds, are saying is that we are in the midst of one of those profound upheavals of society when the fundamentals are being shaken, and a new order emerges. We have seen such times before in the history of Europe, such as during the collapse of the Roman Empire and the birth of Christendom, and the upheavals of the Renaissance and the Reformation. At both times a major shift took place in how the church functioned. Today we need to be ready for a further shift.

It is this which presents the contemporary church with such a challenge. However, it is vital to recognise that the church's task is not simply to understand and to learn to adapt to whatever changes are taking place in the world around us. We are surely also to participate in the shaping of what is emerging. Indeed it is doing that which constitutes the primary mark and purpose of a missionary church. It is called to be a church whose presence is incarnate in the struggles of the surrounding culture. We are not simply called upon to re-order the church so that it survives, but rather so to participate in God's redemption of the whole created order that the church serves his wider purposes in the world.

> *Why are the sufferings of this world so reminiscent of birth pangs (Romans 8)? Because a real birth is occurring. A new creation is about to come to light, a new world is being born.*
> Jose Comblin, *Being Human*, p.173

> *The church may choose to be a spectator at the birth of a new age, but is she not the one midwife capable of bringing forth a safe delivery?*
> MISAG II, *Towards Dynamic Mission*, p.6

We are called to be physicians of that civilisation about which we dream, the civilisation of love.

Pope Paul VI *(31 December 1975)*

Seek the peace and prosperity of the city to which I have carried you into exile. Pray to the Lord for it, because if it prospers, you too will prosper.

Jeremiah 29:7

Such a challenge calls the church to move out of the guard's van, where we are looking back over the distant and disappearing peaks we have passed (or desperately clutching the brake to slow down the pace of change at every point). We are to get out of the guard's van, recover our nerve, and re-discover our true role in the vanguard of society, shaping the new world order in and after the likeness of Christ. Not now, of course, by means of imperial imposition, but rather through incarnate exposition – both of our words and our lives.

The church must be the first sign of what it preaches.

Michael Crosby, *House of Disciples,* p.261

Chapter 2

Understanding pastoral mode

If the church is to make the shift from pastoral to mission mode, as called for by Lambeth 88, then it is important to know what we mean by such terms. It is best not to look for too static a model of either mode, but rather to understand how the church has come to function in pastoral mode, and how it can make the journey into mission mode. When you ask someone to tell you about themselves they will usually tell 'their story'. So too in understanding the pastoral mode of the church, we are most likely to arrive at a true picture by understanding the story (history) of how we came to this point. The following milestones have marked the path which the church has travelled since the days of the catacombs and early centuries of persecution.

The impact of hierarchical societies on the loss of lay vitality

From early on in the Christian era the leadership structures of the church took on a strongly hierarchical form. This reflected the widespread hierarchical nature of surrounding cultures epitomised in the imperial style of the Roman empire, and the subsequently derived feudal system of English culture. Whilst church and leadership structures need to relate to surrounding culture, its calling is to do so in ways that preserve the distinctive nature of the faith community. However, the imperial – and in a double sense 'imposing' – approach to leadership had the effect of making the laity second-class citizens and passive clients (or, in today's terminology 'consumers') of the priestly professionals.

One of the signs of the vitality of the church in the twentieth century has been the recovery of the foundational role of laity, expressed alike in concepts such as 'every member ministry', and in the development of synodical structures of government. However, the church continues to be shaped by a concept of ministry inherited more from our cultural journey, than from the setting off point of the New Testament church with a sense of a whole community being energised and equipped by the Spirit to be the Body of Christ.

The future will certainly entail a continued re-working of the imperial distortions of leadership, and rediscovery of all leadership as servant leadership. The financial constraints in which the church finds itself at present can be seen as divine shaping of the church to recover its Body nature, in a release of the creativity of the whole church. Certainly collaborative styles of leadership, and permission-giving styles of ministry, are marks of local churches which show evident vitality across the churchmanship spectrum.

Such a shift from imperial to servant mode is not only essential for the health of the inner life of the local church, but is essential for the church's engagement in mission. The history of mission is tragically scarred by an imperial style, most gruesomely evident in the Crusades. Today's culture will not hear any message, however good and life-changing, which is communicated to it through any form of coercion, command or claim to authority. In the present debate about disestablishment it is noteworthy that arguments put forward for a retention of some form of established church are essentially about how it is the best way in which the church can *serve* the nation. Power to command has been relinquished.

The shift from Celtic to Roman mode and the loss of community dynamic

This involved the institutionalising of the church into a parish structure, rather than the more fluid and mobile style of the Celtic mission to people-groups. While there are clear gains from a settled geographical area of responsibility and mission, we need to recognise the down-side, namely that the sense of community is lost in the awareness of the institutional perception of the local church. 'Community' is a word associated in Christian vocabulary with monasticism, and religious orders, not with the parish church.

> *For most people, the church is one voluntary association alongside others, one of the many clubs or societal institutions to which they choose to belong. Further, we commonly think of Christian life from an individualistic or, at best, an organisational perspective, but rarely from a communal perspective.*
> John Westerhoff III, *Living the Faith Community*, p.10

There are institutional aspects of the church, but we distort the nature of the faith community if we make those aspects the primary or sole way of seeing the church. Most churches today are not in this sense 'communities'. The development of home groups has been a move within the church to restore the relational element in the life of the church. However, all too often we have to admit that what started as a 'new way of being church' has degenerated into a whole new set of meetings to attend.

11

This institutional overlay of church life tends to create a 'membership mentality' which distorts the very nature of the faith and of discipleship, not least in the 'gathered church' approach.

> *The notions of membership, with club-like connotations of attendance, payment and involvement, only serve to maintain the institutional perception of the contemporary church to which many are allergic. The term is exclusive, with the church building being the equivalent of the bowling club-house, for use by paid up members only. The recovery of the call to be disciples of Jesus Christ carries with it the richness of relationship and the challenge of the dynamic notion of 'following', as people on a journey rather than people who have arrived at some kind of destination.*
>
> Peter Neilson, *Evangelism for Today's Church,* training module

The Reformation loss of a missionary perspective

> *Lutheran orthodoxy believed that the 'Great Commission' had been fulfilled by the apostles and was no longer binding on the church.*
>
> David Bosch, *Transforming Mission,* p.249

Nearer to home, the Church of England was conceived as a church in pastoral mode, and has grown that way since its earliest days. It is a church which does not have its own creed or faith formula, but, rather, claims that its doctrine is in its liturgy – *lex orandi, lex credendi*: the word spoken is the word believed. So when we enquire of the *Book of Common Prayer* about the Church of England's doctrine of evangelism we find that the only reference to evangelism is in the Preface of the 1662 book. There it is explained that the service for the Baptism of those of Riper Years was introduced as 'always useful for the baptising of Natives in our Plantations'. This is not an adequate theology of evangelism for the church at the end of the twentieth century! Whatever the validity of the setting of the church in 1662, we certainly cannot now begin from the notion that church and society are coterminous.

The Enlightenment worldview and the marginalising of values

> *The success of science also precipitated a religious crisis. As the physical evidence for religion was stripped away by successive generations of scientists, faith turned inwards to find a safe refuge inside the self.*
>
> Bryan Appleyard, *Understanding the Present,* p.227.

This has meant that the church, and individuals in it, are reluctant to 'bring God into . . . life, even church life'. The story of a Christian in hospital, suffering from cancer, clearly illustrates this marginalising tendency. She said that half the ward fled when the chaplain came. However, the other half stayed hoping he would come and talk with them about 'ultimate' and 'spiritual' issues, and their fear of death which they did not want to 'burden or embarrass' their family with. Sadly, although he did have a word with them all, he restricted himself to social chat at which he was very skilled. Religion is marginalised and privatised in Enlightenment culture. If that is true of the paid 'purveyors of religion', how much more is it often true of the 'silent adherents'.

> *Many of us today live in a kind of inner apartheid. We segregate out a small corner of pious activities and then can make no sense out of the rest of our lives.*
>
> Richard Foster, *Prayer*, p.179

This marginalising and privatising of values, and beliefs, has also resulted in a fragmentation of life in which different aspects of life are locked in sealed compartments impervious to impact on each other. For some in the church this has resulted in an inability to find any words with which to convey to 'outsiders' the faith enjoyed 'within'. Matthew Fox argues that this separation between personal reality and religion is a major cause of the church losing so many young people today. He writes:

> *It is essential to remember that spirituality is praxis, the praxis of religion. So much of religion in overdeveloped countries is in books, academic institutions, degrees, sermons, and words. While learning is certainly essential to healthy religion, it is no substitute for praxis. Thinking about God is no substitute for tasting God, and talking about God is no substitute for giving people ways of experiencing God. 'Civil' or institutional religion can go on with little spiritual practice but eventually church attendance declines as people begin to find church less meaningful and less interesting than the entertainment that secular society provides. Fewer and fewer persons are attracted to Christianity in the 'First World' countries because there is so little practice, so little spirituality in religion.*
>
> Matthew Fox, *Creation Spirituality*, p.75/6

The loss of distinctives in the twentieth-century Western church

When the end of term report comes to be written on the church in the West in the twentieth century, it will have to include, on the negative side, the phrase 'failure of nerve'. There has been a serious loss of argument with the Enlightenment worldview. The critical approach to scripture, psychology and evolution all found the church unable to stem the tide of a secular, materialistic worldview as the framework in which the people of our culture see reality.

> *What is striking about the books which were written, especially during the eighteenth century, to defend Christianity against these attacks, is the degree to which they accept the assumptions of their assailants.*
>
> Lesslie Newbigin, *The Gospel in a Pluralist Society*, p.3

There has been a consequent loss of gospel content in such evangelism as has been attempted. William Abraham describes the weakness in these terms:

> *At the very best, most modern evangelism hands over two things: deeply reduced fragments of the Christian message and the personalistic debris of the Christian moral tradition.*
>
> William Abraham, *The Logic of Evangelism*, p.141

In similar vein, Richard Lovelace writes:

> *Evangelism-in-Depth and two-by-two house evangelism can expand the trade routes of the gospel outside our church walls, but unless what we export is more than a two-dimensional caricature of Christian spirituality, we will not overcome the credibility gap among consumers.*
>
> Richard Lovelace, *Dynamics of Spiritual Life*, p.236

Moreover, this failure of nerve has been seen in the loss of Christian distinctives and the essentially counter-culture nature of the faith. Yet the very subversive nature of acknowledging Jesus as Lord was crucial to the church's evangelisation of the Roman empire. Today's church member is always eager to show that 'Christians are normal, that Christians can have fun, that Christians can . . .' Valid and understandable though such sentiments are they are strikingly different from Paul's call to the Ephesians (Ephesians 4:17-19), or the words of Jesus (Matthew 5:11-16). Those passages positively celebrate the difference knowing God makes to personal moral values, and lifestyle. A missionary church, though deeply

14

involved in the whole of society, will yet be courageously distinctive from it. It will see itself as called to live by prophetic counter-values.

The point is well illustrated by the blandness of the contemporary church's use of the Lord's prayer as compared with its perception and use in the early centuries of the church's life:

> *Allegiance to the empire was determined by proclaiming the kingship of the emperors, the holiness of their names, and submission to their will. To declare otherwise, as demanded by praying the Our Father, was to act subversively towards the powers and principalities.*
> Michael Crosby, *Thy Will be Done: Praying the Our Father as subversive activity*

Conclusion

Having traced some of the major shaping events that have produced the church as we know it today, we can better identify some of the key marks of the church in pastoral mode. It is a deeply *clerical* structure. That is likely to be a dangerous and inefficient model in a situation where the number of clergy is continuing to decline and – owing to financial constraints – may have to decline further. Unless a compensating change, in the relationship between the respective roles of clergy and laity takes place, then decline in church life must inevitably continue. The church in pastoral mode functions primarily as an *organisation* rather than community. In a culture where all institutions (churches, political parties, unions, etc) are in decline, this way of working is already alienating to the young who function more through networks than institutions. The pastoral mode also has the effect of creating a *'church-life focus'* which does not easily connect with the pressing 'whole-life issues' which dominate modern culture. Such a style tends to create an Ark, rather than the incarnational model of church life. Moreover the pastoral model tends to create a church geared to *comfort*, in what J.K. Galbraith has called 'The culture of contentment'. In the final issue such an approach, geared to keeping people happy rather than making them holy, is not particularly pastoral. The end result is that:

> *Most of us still live in the refuge of our parishes, which are more the relics of an antiquated Christianity than the first fruits of a new people won for Christ in the midst of today's world.*
> Jose Comblin, *Being Human*, p.26

The result of this two thousand year process of shaping the church we have inherited is that the model currently being practised by the church is assumed to be the only way in which the church is to be church. However, other ways of being church have existed during the history of the church, and do exist today. Once that is grasped, we can begin to ask whether the model that we are using is the best that is available, whether other models should be encouraged alongside the existing pattern, and how the way the church currently functions can be re-shaped along the lines of a missionary church.

Here, the sheer dogged endurance of many clergy, and the long-term faithfulness of many congregations and church members may be masking the fact that the church is operating in a mode ill-suited to today's culture. Are we wise to show our courage and determination to keep rowing against an ebb tide which is carrying us out to sea, when there is an on-shore breeze and an outboard motor to hand?

Two ways of being a pastoral church need to be highlighted at this point. One is the *passive pastoral mode* – the maintenance mentality of many congregations simply seeking to 'keep things going'. It involves a surrender to the tide of events.

There is also an *activist pastoral mode* in which all that is involved in keeping the present pattern going has, added to it, anxious activity in an attempt to stem the tide by rowing harder. A missionary congregation is not such an activist pastoral congregation. Rather it is a profound reworking of the whole way of being church which results in proclaiming the gospel as much by how it is the church (being) than by what it does (doing). It is to consideration of this way of being a missionary congregation that we now turn.

Chapter 3

Defining the missionary mode

Having sought to critique the present and predominantly 'pastoral' mode of the church, it is important now to define the nature of the journey which the church will need to make if it is to become a missionary church. That must begin with the church's mission and gospel.

Restoring purpose to the nature of the church

'Why' is one of the most fundamental questions of humanity, from the enquiry of the toddler forever asking 'why', through Hamlet's wrestling with the 'slings and arrows of outrageous fortune', to theologians and philosophers throughout history. Yet the culture in which we live has tended to concentrate so much on the 'how' questions that 'why' questions have not been raised. It is also one of the tendencies of institutions, to forget their purpose in the midst of much effort to ensure their survival. But the 'why' questions are determinative of 'how' survival takes form.

The church is called upon to be a model of how a community is held together by an understanding of its purpose. Revelation gives to the Christian an authentic basis for addressing ultimate questions. The church must reflect the fact that it is a community committed to a particular answer to the question of why we, and the universe, are here – in this form.

Journey is one of the themes that has come to prominence in Christian thinking. It underlines the process nature of the Christian life, and all learning. It has enabled Christians to rediscover and return to their roots (or is it 'routes'?). It has also helped us find our present location on the map of contemporary life. However, the single most important aspect of any journey is the destination. Although it is the last place you get to on the journey, it is the first place to think about, for it dictates the time of departure, the means of travel, and the nature of the resources needed for that journey. Any journey, therefore, starts with consideration of the end. Purpose is inextricably linked to destination. That is why the recovery of purpose will entail putting last things first.

This recovery of purpose in the life and inner structure of the church has a potentially prophetic dimension in a culture which has lost hope – beyond the hope of an upturn in the economy which is hardly a sufficient life-enhancing purpose for those who are part of 'comfortable Britain' and is certainly not sufficient for the growing number of people who through various causes are cut off from the material well-being of the rest.

Two particular focal points of purpose for the church stand out.

End Times

The New Testament is consistent in describing the times in which we live as the End Times and Last Days. This does not mean primarily that chronologically the clock is almost at midnight, but rather that the character of the times in which the church lives is shaped by the End. Sadly eschatology has often to be described as 'the last things we think about', rather than 'what we think about the last things'. Today's culture is in particular need of beginning at the End. Much of the violence in youth culture stems from a lack of purpose, significance, meaning and hope among young people today. For we live without hope, direction, or purpose. The End Times point us to purpose, to the *gathering up* of all things in Christ: *creation, culture* (the nations bringing their wealth before the Lamb), *history, humanity* and the *church* (as the Bride of the True Humanity and second Adam).

The Christian community is to order its life around the values of the Age to Come. It is a community which celebrates, demonstrates, and thereby proclaims the gathering up of all creation in the purposes of God revealed in Christ. It is this vision of the End, and thus of what is of lasting importance, incarnate in human experience, through the word of the kingdom, which expresses the Presence of the Future, and equips the church to participate in God's mission in the world, to redeem the whole creation.

Missio dei

Take a typical book on church life and you are likely to find that 'mission' is where it ends. It is the last chapter. The idea behind this is that 'when we get the church right it will naturally be a missionary church'. This 'overflow' principle does not seem to be working well. If we take the incarnation seriously, then the first way in which we 'get the church right' is to participate in God's mission in the world. David Bosch, in *Transforming Mission*, has defined the emerging ecumenical missionary paradigm as one shaped primarily by participation in the *missio dei*, God's already up-and-running activity in the whole of creation. The key text for such a paradigm is 'God so loved the *world* . . .' (my italics, but maybe his as well!). The church finds its meaning and purpose by discerning and participating in God's mission in the world.

18

Rightly understood, this is to what the historic Creeds point the church. Too easily they are described simply in terms of a series of heresy-resistant dogmas. They are, however, primarily a distillation of the story of scripture (for a non-literate, non-book, culture). As such they describe the purposes of God in terms of his self-disclosure as the Alpha and Omega of all that is. His purposes give meaning and significance to where we came from and to where we are going. God's purposes define humanity's call to participate in his eternal purpose of gathering up everything into Christ (Ephesians 1:10, Colossians 1:20, 1 Corinthians 15:28). Moreover, to be a Christian is to be in Christ, and to be in Christ is to participate in incarnate mission as a mediator of God's presence in the world (Luke 3:22).

One of the liberating effects of the restoration of purpose is a reduction of activity and organisational structure. Without purpose everything should be attempted by the clergy and laity. Once a clear understanding of the purpose of the church universal is grasped, and the nature of the task of the local expression of that purpose, other things fall into place. The good news about the missionary church is that although its path may be more costly, its tasks may well be more limited, and its life a liberation from attempting the impossible agendas that so easily afflict all organisational structures in Western society.

Restoring spirituality to the heart of Christian community

The usual view of the church can be expressed by three interlocking circles which illustrate the areas of *worship* (how we relate to God), *community* (by which is meant the 'faith community', and how we handle relationships within the life of the church), and *mission* (how we engage with the surrounding culture). Important though each of these elements is, there is a crucial area of overlap between all three, at the centre of figure one (see overleaf). It is this area that makes the difference. It is the heart of the church's life, namely its spirituality. By 'spirituality', is meant *'our understanding and experience of how encounter with God takes place and how such an encounter is sustained.'*

figure one: the dynamic of spirituality in the local church

The state of this 'heart' is the crucial factor in the effectiveness of any local church. It is this which explains why two churches, which outwardly seem so similar, can have such different expressions of life. One shares its faith, is growing, gives generously, pays its quota, and exudes a sense of inner vitality expressed in an outwards-directed mentality. The other is numerically static at best, complains about the quota, seems lifeless and is often turned in on itself. The difference has to do with spirituality. This is the heart that pumps life into all that takes place. This being so, the task must be to help churches develop their spiritual life so as to enable them to express it through their worship, community, and mission.

Churches can fail at several points in this process. Some simply do not have a spirituality. The church is a hive of activity, but essentially a hollow shell. There is nothing at the heart. Some have a spirituality, but because it is not clear or spelt out, it is very difficult for anyone to buy into the underlying ('incipient'?) vitality of the place. Yet others have a spirituality which is clear, but does not function as a strong source of vitality because the church has inherited, held on to, or developed, patterns of worship, community and mission that are unconnected with (or do not appropriately express) the spirituality at the heart of the church.

Too often the situation is that worship is in gridlock, fellowship is a tangled skein of wool rather than a network of loving relationships, mission is seen as the work of a few enthusiasts each cutting across the efforts of the others, and spirituality is simply a puzzle. However, there are churches with a clear spirituality that is well expressed in, and reinforced by, the way it handles its worship, community and mission. Such churches are missionary in nature.

Recovering the prophetic dynamic of the gospel

Whenever the church has made significant impact in mission, it has clothed the gospel in a way which resonates with the concerns, needs and aspirations of the surrounding community. Classically we can see this in the work of St Augustine of Hippo. The Greek gods (who were so capricious and unpredictable), and the Roman astrological powers (whose predictions were so fatalistic) had both lost credibility. Augustine pointed rather to the Judeo-Christian God as a God of history and purpose. He gave people hope by participating in God's purposes in the world. It 'rang true', and a considerable 'people-movement' resulted, as well as a whole civilisation based on Christian principles – Western civilisation. Augustine spoke of *purpose*.

Similarly Wesley, in his emphasis on the new birth, gave hope to the oppressed labouring class.

Today we talk about 'enculturating' the gospel. We can equally well speak of incarnating the message. The question is, 'what is that clothed, enculturated gospel for 21st century humanity?' It is a vital question. Bernard Pawley, a former Archdeacon of Canterbury, addressing General Synod in 1979 when the Nationwide Initiative in Evangelism was being launched, said:

> *The long suffering clergy do not wish to be told again and again to reinterpret the gospel or make it relevant; they want help in doing it and want to hear what the gospel sounds like and looks like when it has been so treated. There is therefore here a poverty of inspiration which I find a little alarming. It seems to me at this point the whole enterprise betrays its lack of inspiration and needs to be reorientated in one particular classical direction, that of prophecy. If you are going to indulge in evangelism, you have got to have prophets, who to my mind are signally lacking. If you want to do evangelism, first catch your prophet.*

Bernard Pawley, *Report of Proceedings, July 1979*, p.514

My thesis at this point is that 'what the gospel sounds like and looks like when it has been so treated' is essentially about our *being human*. The

Good News, as it relates to our culture, is that being fully human has been demonstrated for us in the person of Jesus Christ, made accessible to us through baptismal incorporation into his death, resurrection, ascension and the gift of the Holy Spirit, and is now being incarnately demonstrated at your nearest local church (or should be). *The prophetic word for our culture is about what it means to be human.*

Space does not permit further exploration of the nature of being human, beyond the following brief comments. First, the doctrine of the Trinity points us to the fact that we are beings-in-relationship, rather than creatures complete in ourselves. Second, Genesis, in pointing to our being made in the image of God, indicates that we are called to participate in his creativity, in his celebration (Day Seven), and community with him who is Community. Third, the whole of scripture points to the fact that life is made possible and sustained in existence, by grace. Living eucharistically – with an attitude of thanksgiving for the gift of life – is central to what it means to be human. In short, some of the key parameters of what it means to be fully human, is to be a eucharistic, creative and celebratory community, and a participator in God's purposes for the whole of his creation.

Human society has been through various revolutions, the agricultural, industrial, technological, and information revolutions have come ever more closely on each other's heels. Yet in the midst of it all we have lost any solid sense of who and why we are.

> *The paradox is that all of science's 'truths' and the 'real' world are based upon the most flagrant distortion. In creating an understandable universe, we have committed ourselves to the most gross and obvious oversimplification. We have excluded the understanding mechanism, the self . . .*
> Bryan Appleyard, *Understanding the Present,* p.208/9

This has resulted in a sense of 'moral and spiritual vacuum at the heart of our society' which was somehow brought to the surface in our own country by the manner of the death of James Bulger. It was deeply symbolic, for it was the story of a child lost in the market place. We have lost our 'inner child' (the capacity to wonder, to live in the present, to enjoy life – as gift rather than product or purchase) in our pursuit of possessions. Our whole society is in danger of dying from consumption.

In this sense of lostness humanity has turned in on the self (*'incurvatus in se'*, as St Augustine defined sin). The self that was lost, excluded and ignored in Enlightenment culture has risen again in narcissistic consumer society. Our culture is lost at sea, and has thrown away the (Christian) charts of how to find our true home and centre.

22

The Consumer Society is . . . a flight from human vulnerability, through a channelling of human desire into the amassing of possessions.

John Kavanaugh, *Still Following Christ in a Consumer Society*, p.4

Recovering the truth that Christianity is about 'being human' is both good news for Western society, and a definition of its agenda, that many in and beyond the church have come to recognise and which St Irenaeus affirmed long ago, that 'the glory of God is a man fully alive'.

The great work of our time is for Western man to put his own inner house in order. E.F. Schumacher, *Small is Beautiful*

Salvation is, essentially considered, the restoration of humanity to man. James Philip, *Christian Maturity*, p.70

God is not about religion, and very much religion, I fear, is not about God. God is about the fulfilment of being human and personal in the glory and celebration of the community of love . . . We are invited to join in on God's universal project of sharing and developing love. David Jenkins, *Good God!*, lecture 4, p.3

The application of the gospel to contemporary Western culture is, I submit, participation in the search for our lost humanity. *The mission of the church is to participate in the 'human project'.*

If the recovery of purpose is likely to lead to the simplification of the role of the church, the recovery of the task of being human is likely to be further good news, for it integrates the internal life of the church (the discovery, liberation and celebration of the new humanity opened up by Christ) with its external missionary task (to proclaim the truth and availability of the new humanity made possible by Christ). What we are called to *do*, tell and serve others in their search for our lost humanity, is also what we are called to *be,* those who enjoy and affirm one another in the community of faith as together we make exodus from false values into the wholeness of life made possible through Christ. In this way the whole life of the church becomes at one and the same time both pastoral (building up the faithful) and missionary (proclaiming the faith). Again to hard-pressed clergy and over-stretched laity, this is good news indeed.

Such radical simplification of the purpose and role of the church may well be the paradigm shift which the new cultural setting calls for:

> *Many new intellectual departures have become possible only after the luxuriant complexities accumulated before them have once more been reduced to surveyable simplicity.*
> Peter Berger, *A Rumour of Angels*, p.117

Recovering the baptismal identity of every believer

The loss of Christian distinctives, by which the church is seen to proclaim the gospel through its lifestyle, has a significant diluting effect on the witness of the church. All too often evangelism is simply introducing people to what may be called 'bolt-on spirituality'. By this is meant that people coming to faith are led into some initial encounter with God, but that experience is not properly related to or grounded in the whole life of the person. As a result an experience of God is bolted onto a secular worldview, lifestyle, value system, and personal identity. When testing comes, including the moral decisions which go to make up our experience of life, such a person is likely to make response out of the secular worldview out of which they still function.

Two American writers have expressed this well about the church in America:

> *The contemporary American church is so largely enculturated to the American ethos of consumerism that it has little power to believe or act.*
> Walter Brueggemann, *The Prophetic Imagination*, p.11

> *Just as the identity of a modern American is in part defined by the commitment to life, liberty and the pursuit of happiness, so the identity of those who have entered into the Israel of God is defined by a commitment to pursue love for God and the neighbour.*
> William Abraham, *The Logic of Evangelism*, p.35

Much the same can be said about the church in the whole of the West, including England.

One of the ways of addressing this situation is evidenced in the renewal of the catechumenate, and in the significant shift to a process approach to evangelism whereby people have time and opportunity to engage in a dialogue with the faith and take it into their whole lifestyle. Ways need to be found of evangelising the whole person, establishing the new, and existing, believer in a Christian worldview focused upon the purposes of God, in a Christian identity as baptised into Christ and his filial relationship with the Father, and called to reflect the divine nature and the values of the age to come in the handling of such major areas of life as money, sex and power. Such a church, renewed in the quality of its faith, would find a watching world eager to know more of the source of its joy, faith, courage, justice and love.

As the Archbishops' Commission on Rural Areas affirmed, baptism is the basis of the constitution of the church and its mission. Rightly understood, baptism is the commissioning of the laity into the priestly, prophetic and kingly ministry of Christ. This is the foundational ministry of the church, and shifts the perspective of the believer from one of spectator to participator, and from consumer of, to worker in, God's mission to the world.

This is essentially the work of increasing the *quality* of faith and discipleship in existing members of the church, yet its knock-on effect is likely to stimulate the *quantity* of newcomers. Peter, in his first – and strongly catechetical – epistle writes about evangelism in terms of being ready to give an answer for 'the reason for the hope within us'. It is the lack of evidence of that distinctive hope in the life of much of the church that explains contemporary culture's apathy about asking the questions that really matter.

Renewing the community character of church life

There is no life that is not in community,
And no community not lived in praise of God.
T.S. Eliot, Choruses from 'The Rock'

Humanity, certainly in Western technological society today, is caught between the vastness of the impersonal state and multi-national machinery of society on the one hand, and the loneliness of individualism on the other. The loneliness of the individual, which in the view of Mother Teresa of Calcutta has reached epidemic proportions in the West, is being continually accentuated by the breakdown of the family, and the collapse of natural community.

Into this social vacuum the church is sent in mission. It has the role of restoring natural community, albeit in a different form from previous patterns which have broken down, through the restoration of its own life. It is a life-giving yet costly call, for the art of community making has, rather like the art of drystone walling, become nearly a lost art. In personal social grouping and business structures, networking is today's way of both relating and functioning (being and doing). The church needs to be alive to this, willing and able to encourage the networking of individuals that by-passes the organisational, and courageous enough to let a good number of institutional forms of being church die with dignity.

Particularly as the church seeks to communicate with the under thirties, it must face the fact that they have little vision for or commitment to institutions as such. However, committed to faith in Christ, they have little interest in organisational work. Indeed the significant drop in the number of under twenty-fives coming forward for the ordained ministry may well be due to the perceived institutional nature of the task.

Such a journey into the rediscovery of true community will not be accomplished without major church surgery. All too easily the church, particularly in pastoral mode where Parkinson's law operates in terms of 'needs expand to consume resources available', is a greedy animal. It sucks all life and energy into itself. This is why the shift to a whole life focus is so vital. Only by the recovery of the essential missionary nature of the church will motivation be found to release and resource church members for their life and work outside the organisation and structure of the local church.

As the church makes this shift into community it will find the surrounding community shifting its awareness of what it means by church. That shift can be expressed in terms of the movement from:

> *church = building + priest + stipend*
>
> to
>
> *church = community + faith + action*

A shift from a church life to a whole life focus.

A church effectively engaged in mission will see that participating in the *missio dei* will involve shifting emphasis from a focus on the life of the local church, and a concern to keep everyone in it happy (which too easily passes for 'pastoral concern'), to a concern for the world in its needs, joys and struggles. The work, for example, of engaging with the sick, the grieving and the dying, as well as with the moral issues of such roles in society as those concerned with wealth creation or medical ethics, is indeed pastoral. It is the shift from the maintenance and 'keeping people happy' mode in which the church all too often operates, into engagement with these situations that will bring the church into the pastoral-in-mission mode of operating for which Lambeth 88 called.

It will mean concern not so much for 'the work of ministry' as for 'the ministry of work'. It will be about equipping church members to live out their humanity within the family and the work place (and lack of work) in response to God. Much is already happening here from the work of the *Gospel and Our Culture* movement to the various resources and projects designed to help people with everyday living. Resources include the Board of Education's training course *Monday Matters*, the latest Mothers' Union course *To Live and Work*, and the *Faith in Life* material.

For such a shift to take place, the structures of the local church will need to be simplified, and new priorities adopted. However, much can be done within existing ways of operating. The intercessions each Sunday in public worship give a marvellous opportunity to engage with the hopes and fears of everyday life. Home groups geared outwards to engage with whole-life issues can also contribute significantly. The description of the Christian faith as 'the Way' gloriously expresses this understanding that the faith is not so much about doing different things (for example going to church) there are some such aspects to the faith, as it is about doing things differently.

Senator Gordon Wilson's response of forgiveness for the death of his daughter Marie, killed in the Enniskillen Remembrance Day bombing, stands as a glorious example of the power of someone handling the tragedies of life Christianly. It is this costly call to do things differently, Christianly, which is likely to bring about significant progress in mission, rather than the multiplication of mission events. It was this quality of life which undergirded, and energised, the servant evangelism of the early church.

> *Shortly after Anthony, Pachomius, the other great founder of Egyptian monasticism, established more highly organised communities . . . His initial encounter with Christians came after he had been conscripted into the army. As a cold, hungry, and miserable soldier he was . . . brought food and other necessities, an act of charity which overwhelmed Pachomius . . . [who] was so struck by this that he prayed to God, vowing that if he were allowed to escape, he would become a Christian.*
>
> Roberta Bondi, *To Pray and to Love*, p.18/19

Arguably this one shift might just be sufficient to bring about all the others listed above, certainly it is crucial to the very nature of what it means to be a missionary congregation, and what distinguishes a church in pastoral mode from one in mission mode.

Chapter 4

Can a missionary congregation work?

Before proceeding to consider how missionary congregations might be brought into being, it is necessary to address three fundamental questions about the desirability, and possibility, of turning local churches into missionary congregations.

Are missionary congregations desirable?

The argument here is that one of the great strengths of the Anglican church is that it sees itself as a church to and for the whole community, not as a gathered church. The notion of a missionary congregation, indeed the very word congregation, seems to smack of congregationalism, of a gathered-church, ghetto mentality, and as such a sign of the final withdrawal of the church into the shell of itself and its self-consciousness – all in the name of mission.

Reality is in fact more subtle and potentially more creative. The basis of the parish-church versus gathered-church divide is rooted deeply in the nature of the Christendom/Reformation model of a church coterminous with society, against which the Anabaptists reacted by shaping the church around the gathering of the faithful. History has however moved on since then. Neither of these models, especially in the caricatured form in which they are often presented, is a viable option today. A church that is indistinguishable from the local community, and coterminous with it, is a church that has virtually disappeared from view; it has nothing distinctive about itself, nor any message to speak. Of what value is a church that has nothing to say? Equally a gathered church that is not rooted in, and part of, a local community, although it may well have a strong and distinctive message, actually has no one to address. Of what value is a church that has something vital to say, but no one to say it to?

However, this is a serious challenge to the concept of missionary congregations for it does seem that churches with most vitality do, rather like business organisations with high achievements, require a level of participation which cannot be sustained over the long term. Ironically this is true of the church in *pastoral* mode. It does tend to use all its resources in the sustaining and expansion of its own life. Indeed such churches are rather like red giant stars. Such stars, which are at the end of their life cycle, eject much of their substance in an expanding cloud whilst at the same time shrinking to an inner intense but shrinking core. That is not what a missionary church should be like.

Rather, any church worth its salt (Matthew 5:13) will, like an ellipse, have two focal points. It will be a church that is truly and effectively *engaged* with individuals and with the dynamic of the local community in which the church is set. It will also be *distinctive* within that culture. A missionary congregation will, by definition, be both *distinctive* and *engaged*.

It is worth pointing out that the axis of such an ellipse, with these two focal points, can be seen to highlight some interesting characteristics of local churches. On a rural/urban axis it is soon evident that rural churches find it easier to be engaged and more difficult to be distinctive, whilst urban churches often find it easier to be distinctive yet more difficult to be engaged.

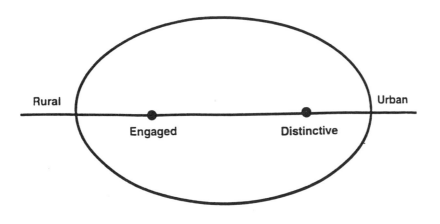

figure two: the engaged/distinctive axis of the church

It is important to note here that a rural church that is appropriately engaged and distinctive will look very different from an urban church that is engaged and distinctive. Furthermore, there are many ways even for different rural (or urban) churches to be appropriately engaged and distinctive. The central axis can also be used to reflect the contrasting tendencies of 'conservative' and 'liberal' churches. Conservative churches find it easier to be distinctive than engaged, and liberal churches easier to be engaged than distinctive. The essential point is that any church that allows itself to be polarised as belonging to a totally gathered or totally dispersed church style will have lost the necessary creative tension of a missionary congregation of being both engaged and distinctive.

Are missionary congregations attainable?

> *To my mind taking the whole congregation into mission is a bit optimistic. For church culture is part of the problem rather than the solution. Churches tend to be homogenous at present. Incarnational mission involves the movement beyond the subcultural boundaries of the church. This is not everyone's calling. Emphasis on a gathered ecclesiology and 'family' ideas about the church have compounded the problem. I sense this behind some of your wish to create missionary congregations.*
>
> Pete Ward, *Archbishop of Canterbury's adviser for youth work (personal letter 29.4.94)*

Certainly, it will not be possible to shift every church. Some are in a terminal state and need to be allowed, indeed helped, to die with dignity. Others are, for the present at least, blocked – often through the hijacking of power within the existing structures. However, I dare to suggest that it is realistic to contemplate achieving a major shift in focus across the board in the life of the church today. Resistance to change is a real obstacle, but it can be overcome. The following factors are positive forces working for such a shift in focus of the average congregation.

(a)   *Survival* may well be the catalyst for change that we need, even if it casts the Church Commissioners in the unlikely role of 'agent of mission'.

(b)   So may the ordination of *women*. Their leadership style could be just what the church needs if it is to engage in the human project. Indeed, anecdotal evidence suggests that it is unusual to find a woman leading a church which is not growing. Such churches may well be growing in *humanity* prior to their growing in *numbers*. Like Esther we may well be right to say to such women, 'Who knows but that you have come to royal position for such a time as this?' (Esther 4:14). Like Deborah, their community building skills may well be the missionary work of the local church to the communities in which the church operates:

> *Village life in Israel ceased,*
> *ceased until I, Deborah, arose,*
> *arose a mother in Israel.*
> Judges 5:7

(c) *Relief* may play a powerful part. In churches that have been struggling to survive in pastoral mode, the discovery that the way ahead is about helping each other to be human, to receive the gift of life, and to share it with others, may come as such overwhelming good news that all sorts of sacrifices and costs will be embraced because of the 'joy that is set before us'.

(d) *Resonance*, in the community. If 'the search for meaning' is at the heart of our human condition today, then once a church embraces this focus for its mission and message, it could well find a people eager to hear. If this is the enculturated gospel there will be a resonance with those around which will speak powerfully. We only need a few such churches, first for the attention of the rest of the church to be turned and then for its agenda to be changed.

(e) *Time*, in a strange way, may be on our side. It could well be that the only churches which will survive over the next couple of decades will be the ones that have embraced the missionary agenda. Those which 'play safe' with the pastoral model may find themselves disappearing.

Yes, a change to a missionary dynamic is a massive shift. It involves the conversion of local churches, but the time is ripe and the 'crisis' sufficient to provoke attention. Certainly groups should be released which are incarnating the gospel, but we should not abandon the attempt to turn the whole ship round.

Are missionary congregations sustainable?

> *You cannot sustain a missionary congregation.*
> *It is like a ring doughnut, there is nothing at the centre.*
>
> John Finney, *former National Officer for Evangelism,*
> *now Bishop of Pontefract*

This is a valid criticism of the 'church for others' approach of the WCC in the 1960s (though there is much valuable insight in what they were saying then which has continuing relevance today). William Temple's famous dictum that 'the church is the only organisation which exists entirely' (or did he mean/say 'primarily') for the benefit of non-members' suffers from the same criticism. 'All mission and no play makes Jack (and Jill) a dull church'; and the converts tend to die young – from exhaustion. If mission is all about 'going out and getting them in', then this is a valid criticism.

Such churches are like shopkeepers who stand outside their shop trying to persuade people to come in. However, they are not being invited in to buy, but rather to help persuade other people to come in, who in turn are not being invited to buy, but to help persuade other people to come in . . . and so on. All the time, there is actually nothing on the shelves to buy. It is a sales-addicted organisation. That is not what is meant by a missionary congregation, and the idea will need to be protected from activists who want to load the church with yet more, and more diverse, tasks.

For this reason, though we can welcome the sentiment we should not subscribe to the notion that 'the church exists by mission as fire exists by burning'. Replace the word 'mission' by 'love', and then we are speaking truth – and pointing to the centrality of the 'human project'. John Finney is right. A church wholly given to 'mission work' is not a sustainable model.

However, and this is a vital point, to define the gospel as entering into the gift of being fully human as demonstrated and made available in Christ does two vital things. Not only does it clothe the gospel for today's culture; it also creates a life-giving interactive loop between being and doing, between church life and mission activity. For a missionary congregation is one which sees its calling as both to be and to tell the good news. It is the community whose life consists in the celebration and enjoyment of the liberating wholeness of Jesus Christ. This is a sustainable model, run on the renewable resources of God's grace, empowered by the alternating currents of giving and receiving the gift of the new humanity. On sale in this shop is the staff, and the stuff, of life. The sales line reads:

> *Come, all you who are thirsty, come to the waters;*
> *and you who have no money, come, buy wine and milk*
> *without money and without cost.*
> *Why spend your money on what is not bread,*
> *and your labour on what does not satisfy?*
> *Listen, listen to me, and eat what is good,*
> *and your soul will delight in the richest of fare.*
> *Give ear and come to me; hear me, that your soul may live.*

> *Isaiah 55:1-3*

Truly, there is jam in the centre of this doughnut!

Chapter 5

How can a missionary congregation work?

In this tumbled present we must build,
for damaged beauty needs a new design.
John Bates, *Damaged Beauty Needs a New Design*

In the light of what has already been expressed, the question which now needs to be addressed is, *'What can and should be done to bring about the shift from pastoral to mission focus in the life of the church?'* There are three aspects to the answer. First, the need for commitment to a fundamental shift in the purpose of the local church needs to be faced, explored and acted upon. Second, it is important to consider ways in which missionary congregations are already, and might increasingly in the future, be structured. Third, we need to consider how a typical parish church might be helped to become a missionary congregation.

Opting for change

Bringing about change is at one level very simple. We need to decide to bring it about. It is that simple, yet the very simplicity makes more stark the radical nature of what is needed. Like the rich young ruler, there is the danger that the sheer richness of the Anglican heritage might cause us to go away sorrowful. For the call to be a missionary church is nothing less than a call to conversion – to metanoia, a change of mind, heart and direction. Only, in this situation, it is a matter of the conversion of a community rather than an individual. It involves the turning around of a whole group to face the mission implications of being Christian. Such change is essentially both simple, and costly.

> *When Christ bids a man come, he bids him come and die.*
> Dietrich Bonhoeffer, *The Cost of Discipleship*

> *No change even from worse to better is ever accomplished without pain.*
> Richard Hooker

So the first, and crisis point (in the sense of a critical decision moment) is that of a church, or at least initially it may be just its leadership, making a commitment of will to seek to become a missionary congregation. It is a decision, though borne of long reflection, that is made in a moment.

33

Yet, without such a decision, no real movement will ever take place. This is the hinge on which the viability of the local church as a missionary congregation lies.

This is a two-fold decision.

It is *commitment to a whole-life focus* for the local church, a shaping of the meaning and purpose of the life of the individual and of the Christian community towards engaging in God's creative and redeeming work with planet earth and its global village. This shift from 'church life' to 'whole life' focus, must shape the style, agenda, and priorities of the church.

With such a commitment to a 'whole-life focus' there also needs to be *a commitment to a counter-culture view of discipleship*. The whole range of images used by Jesus to describe the church – salt, light, yeast – also define the church's relationship to the community in which it is set. Each image, in different ways, points to the distinctive nature of the church. Not that this should be interpreted negatively as withdrawal from society. Rather, the reverse. The church is called to engage *distinctively* in Christ's incarnate mission. This two-fold choice to participate in Christ's mission is well expressed by John Robinson:

> **The Christian style of life is marked by an extraordinary combination of detachment and concern. This Christian will care less for the world and at the same time care more for it than the man who is not a Christian. He will not lose his heart to it, but he may well lose his life for it.**
>
> John Robinson, *On Being the Church in the World,* p.18

Such a choice and change is most likely to come about as churches and their leadership glimpse another order of reality and another way of being church. The vision of the kingdom, and the values and nature of the new creation and the life of the Age to come, are not intended to take us out of the world, but rather to energise us for mission in this world. It is the vision of what could be that is most likely to bring about change of what is. This is why putting 'last things first' is so important. It could well be the primary and most vital episcopal ministry in today's church, to give such a vision of what will be and could be, that churches and individuals will opt for change into mission mode.

Opting for which change

In all that has been said so far it could be argued that there are two different senses in which the church is being presented 'in mission mode'. One, whose keynote is *distinctive*, is focused on the church's inner life and the way in which the church is called to model a 'counter-value community'. The other, whose keynote is *missio dei*, is focused on the church engaging with God's activity in the world – participating in what God is doing already.

Both are essential elements in the mission of the church. What is important is that they are integrated. That happens when the church can discern the prophetic word that God desires to speak into a situation or culture and then is able both to live that word and participate in bringing it into being in the surrounding community.

One example of the integration of these two aspects is the church in South Africa in recent years. It was able to discern the essentially de-humanising effect of apartheid, and to see that equality was a primary mark of the *missio dei* in that culture. It repented of its own practice and support of apartheid, sought to adopt a different ('distinctive') set of valuation of all human life, preached the message of equality, and partic-ipated in the political debate and action that brought about the funda-mental change we have recently witnessed.

A similar pattern and story can be seen in the changes that have taken place in many of the countries of Eastern Europe, and the role of the church in bringing about those changes.

It is in the discernment of the prophetic dimension of the Christian message, that the church finds the integration of these two aspects of its missionary nature.

Options for change

Once a commitment to become a missionary church has been made, or indeed as an aid to making that decision, consideration needs to be given as to the ways in which such changes might be expressed. Here our start-ing point must be to establish the fact that there are many alternatives. Such a notion is in conflict with the conventional wisdom that our present way of operating, namely the normal parish church, is the only way of being church. If modern philosophers are saying that 'there are no meta-narratives now' (no overarching ways of describing the whole of reality) so also there may well be no 'meta-way' of being church.

> *There are many possible forms of church life in modern society and no one form is normative.*
> The Church for Others (WCC Report, 1967) p.83

In a period of transition we would be wise to 'let a thousand flowers bloom'. Only ten may be found to be viable in the emerging climate, but only by working that way can we discover which they are. Incidentally, it would give us nine more ways of being church than we have now. That may seem a rather wasteful way of proceeding. It is not that there will be literally one thousand new ways of being church. What is being argued is the encouragement of variety and diversity. Some such 'experiments' will fail, but their value will be in pointing to what will be needed, so they have their place. Others will be right but just for a short period. Others will give us lasting models of change. In a culture where all institutions (Trade Unions, Political Parties, Royalty, etc) are at a disadvantage, we would certainly be wise not to put all our eggs in the institutional basket.

This will mean releasing groups within churches to find different ways of being church, within the total framework of the local church. It will also mean affirming those who are functioning beyond the local church. It was Wesley's desire to develop 'new ways of being church' which caused the needless division into Methodism. The church today needs the largeness of mind and heart to avoid repeating that error in its handling of new manifestations of vitality today. The first shoots of such a shift are already evident in a number of developments.

Emerging patterns

In this brief survey, we start with the most radical, and move – as in a spectrum – towards a way of being a missionary congregation which any parish church could adopt. The range of this spectrum is represented in the diagram below.

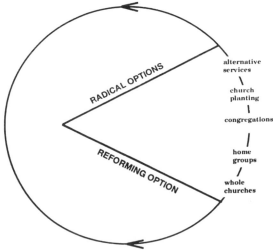

figure three: a fresh angle on being church today

'*Alternative services*' are emerging, and the term means something quite different from *The Alternative Service Book 1980*. There are forms of being church emerging, particularly out of youth culture, which are evidence of new ways not just of worshipping, but of being church. Among such developments are Holy Disorder (Gloucester), Joy (Oxford), the Nine O'Clock Service (Sheffield) and the Late Late Service (Glasgow). Non-youth developments of other ways of being church can be seen in the exploration of an English form of Base Communities, and in a number of UPA ventures.

These developments need to be monitored, encouraged, and helped to avoid the dangers of their own overdeveloped individuality. The latter point is important as history reminds us that a good number of groups and churches which have set off on the journey into mission mode, have become lost and sidetracked on the way. However, it is vital that the journey is made. Whole new expressions of church life are important for one way of making the shift from pastoral to mission mode, is to 'begin all over again'. This is not best done by abandoning the tradition and heritage of the Church of England, but rather by having freedom to reinterpret it in a way that speaks to today's culture. Permission for creative alternatives is an important part of the way ahead.

Church planting is another model for developing missionary congregations. While some church plants are simply ways of having 'more of the same', and others are trapped in a modernist mode that is likely to bear little fruit, a good number are missionary congregations. As such they need the support and encouragement of the wider church.

'*Congregations*' is a concept emerging with a new meaning in the church today. A number of parish churches now function in 'congregations'. By this is meant that each congregation is seen as a distinct grouping, often geared to mission to a particular cultural group. For many decades the 'eight o'clockers' (those who only attend a said, usually BCP, form of Communion early on Sunday) have been difficult to integrate with the rest of the worshipping community. However, there is now a shift from seeing that every service should reflect the whole of the styles of worship appropriate to the context and spirituality of the local congregation, to a more diverse approach. When such diversity (itself a mark of Anglicanism) is embraced, ways can then be found to hold together several distinct worshipping communities within the one church. Such diversity used to be resisted at all costs. More recently it has become a fact of life that even the clergy seem powerless to avoid. Increasingly, churches are seeing that the encouragement of such diversity is a way of 'working with the grain' of our diverse culture. For a number of churches, allowing and assisting one (possibly new) congregation to develop on consciously 'missionary' lines may also be the best way around entrenched attitudes.

Home groups are, for many churches, likely to be a fruitful seed bed for new developments, for they enable groups within churches, committed to the missionary endeavour of the church, to re-shape the way they operate, and especially their 'whole-life orientation', whilst being fully part of the local parish church. There is today, in some churches, a growing struggle with home groups – and a feeling that they may have reached their 'sell by' date. The re-focusing of their life around the missionary nature of the church could be a life-giving step. The principles of the section above on 'defining the missionary mode' certainly apply as fully to a home group as to a whole congregation. Much can be achieved by groups being given permission to explore these issues. They will either provide ways in which the whole church can go, or salutary lessons to protect the whole church from change which can go wrong.

Work groups are groups of people who come together because of the secular work they are involved in. This is one vital and creative way in which the church can adopt a 'whole-life focus'. Christians involved, for example, in working in the internal market of the Health Service need to discern together how Christian values apply to their work.

It may well be that such groups draw people together from more than one church, either because there are not enough of such people in any one church, or because the group is drawn from – for example – the staff of one particular hospital. Seeing such groups as truly church groups should mean that the local church can support and affirm those involved – and not overload them with 'local church' tasks.

Church life aspects point to the place for the missionary nature of the church to be applied to different aspects of the church's life in turn – rather than attempting a total renewal in one thrust. So, for example, attention could be paid to the spirituality or worship of the church first, and then the community and mission structures tackled later. In this way many lessons can be learned and a significant amount of pain and disappointment avoided, though certainly not entirely.

Whole churches. Stimulating though the creative alternatives to the parish church are, the primary work of building missionary congregations must lie in bringing about the renewal of the normal parish church.

The long-term goal, and certainly the primary focus of this paper, is the shifting of the normal parish church from pastoral to mission mode. This is a longer, harder, slower work than that of encouraging radical new developments, a good number of which are of course also likely to be part of a parish church making this shift. It is important to affirm the flexibility of the parochial system to encompass such changes. A structure which, in this century, has adapted to lay involvement in leadership through the introduction of PCCs, the subsequent development of synodical government, sweeping liturgical change, heightened financial responsibility, the spread of multi-benefice parishes, and many other changes, should be able to make this shift too.

If the whole church can follow this path then it will find its options continually expanding. This expansion is represented by the dotted line which completes the circle in *figure three* above (page 36). As alternative patterns emerge out of the church looking for *radical options* so the forms and number of ways in which the church is church will expand. Equally, as the church pursues the *reforming option* by seeking to help every parish church to become a missionary congregation so too the range of healthy (distinctive -and-engaged) churches will grow. By the grace of God such a process will actually result in the radical options looking increasingly like parish churches, and parish churches looking more like healthy and creative expressions of the radical option.

If the radical new initiatives are the tugs that will get the liner out of harbour, then the reformation of the existing ways of being church is about the building of the liner. The one is dependent on the other. Tugs are an inefficient way of transporting a thousand or so passengers across the Atlantic; that is not their task. Equally, liners may run aground before they ever leave harbour unless they learn to seek the help of tugs. Yet, in the final issue the primary focus of this whole paper is on the greater and larger task of 'turning the whole ship round'; in other words, helping every parish church to become a missionary congregation. All that follows is addressed, in the first place, to making the shift from pastoral to mission mode in the local church, though the principles apply equally to new initiatives as well.

Global models

The WCC report *The Church for Others* (1967), speaks of the church needing to break out of 'morphological fundamentalism'. This marvellous phrase refers to the tendency in any organisation to consider the present way of doing things as the only, and necessarily the best, way of doing things. At any time this is a foolish posture. In a culture of rapid change, and in a period of profound transition, this could well prove fatal. Structures have little or no validity in and of themselves. They exist to achieve certain things. They are to be measured by how effective they are in achieving the particular purpose for which they are designed.

The history of liturgical development shows the necessity of change as well as the resistance to it. Cranmer's development of the radical novelty of a liturgy in English should remind us that the Church of England began in life with a radical and creative innovation. The ASB has been adopted, although with some resistance, yet in a remarkably short time and widespread way. One dares to believe Cranmer would, in our day, have been a great supporter of such liturgical change. Yet over this period the way of 'being church' has lacked any parallel development. The geographical equation has continued in terms of: *church = building + priest + stipend.*

There are alternatives. Some may be better ways of doing the job – of being the church to a whole nation. Much of the defence of the parochial system and structure is founded on the healthy instinct not to 'withdraw to the middle-class areas'. However, that is then used to block all thought of exploring whether the above formula is the best or only way. The international church has much to teach us at just this point. Three different models can be highlighted to show that other models do exist, are working remarkably well, and deserve consideration as models that can be incorporated into the ways of being church in England today.

(a) An African model

It is not infrequent for a priest in Africa to be responsible for fifteen to twenty congregations in one parish. A number of such congregations will be recent 'church plants' established by lay evangelists. In some dioceses nearly a third of funds is allocated to employing such evangelists. It inevitably requires a higher role for lay leadership in every congregation. It is certainly a dynamic and missionary structure. Integrating the role of priest and evangelist as well as marrying the work of church planting and the parish system, certainly seem to have valuable insights for the church in England.

(b) A North American model

Though not strictly a 'church' model, it has much to say to the Christian church. The model is that of Alcoholics Anonymous. It is a form of exodus community in which self-help groups enable each other to break out of alcoholic and other addictions.

Its relevance to the life of the church can well be illustrated by the fact that there are currently 25,000 participants in AA groups in the UK. That is about the same number of people as are on the electoral roll of an average-sized diocese. Such a diocese would have an annual salary bill of around £3.5m. AA in England has an annual salary bill of around

£40,000. Their only employed staff are three secretarial staff in the headquarters offices.

(c) A South American model

The Base Communities of the Roman Catholic church are also lay-led groupings of the church. There are around 80,000 such groups now, serviced by comparatively few priest/facilitators (delightfully called 'animators'). As Leonardo Boff, in his book *Ecclesiogenesis* has pointed out, the traditional church model functions on the vertical axis of priest-sacrament, while base communities function on the horizontal axis of word-laity. Base Communities, like AA groups, are also 'exodus communities' enabling people to break free not so much from individual and personal addictions, as from corporate and cultural oppression and corruption. Some we might judge, from our Western/Northern stance, are overly politicised, but most are creative celebrations of hope and community in a setting of poverty, fear and injustice. The church in England is badly in need of communities that will model a way of life which liberates from the crushing of the human spirit inflicted by the consumer culture. Our problem, which perhaps explains why Base Communities have had relatively little success in the UK, is that the 'oppressive' nature of consumer culture is not evident to us – and we find it rather attractive. We do not want to be freed.

None of the these models are held up as *the* answer. However, together they do the more important task of alerting us to the fact that the familiar is neither the only, or necessarily the best. They prompt us to seek liberation from morphological fundamentalism into creative new ways of being church in our unique setting.

Taking things forward

This paper represents a first step in identifying the issue of seeing the church as the primary agent of mission. The next stage of helping to build missionary congregations will involve identifying already existing missionary congregations (using the criteria of this paper) with a view to discovering how the shift from pastoral to mission mode took place. It will then be important to develop ways of helping a wider circle of churches to make the same journey. It may well be that study programmes and packages will not be sufficient on their own to bring about such a paradigm shift. It will be important to consider the roles both of facilitators and of local church leaders (ordained and lay) and how their contribution can best be made to enable the local church to become a missionary congregation.

Frameworks for change

This opting for change is essentially the work of a moment, it is a crisis moment – a time of *choosing*. But choices lead to consequences, and opting for mission leads straight into the *process of changing*. Churches will not, and do not become missionary congregations overnight. Five to ten years is much more likely to be the actual time scale in which to shift the fundamentals and lay new foundations. This period is akin to the catechumenate of a church community. It will be followed by a lifetime of living out the full consequences. In the initial foundation-laying stage the very duration of time is itself likely to play a crucial part. Holding onto the vision when it does not seem to be working, or when seemingly impossible obstacles stand in the way, is a vital part of the maturing of the church, and the refining of its leadership and members (see my book *On the Anvil*). It is both salutary and encouraging to remember that

> **'Most people overestimate what they can achieve in one year, and underestimate what they can achieve in five years'.**

In this process it is likely that a church, and its leadership, committed to making such a change, will benefit from the help of a facilitator/consultant /soul-friend. Such change is not easy, and the help of someone alongside can be of advantage in the battles and puzzles that are likely to be faced. A major part can be played by dioceses as they help churches face the need to become missionary in nature, and by making resources available to facilitate the process of becoming a missionary church.

The work of facilitating itself needs a suitable framework within which to operate, as does the task of leadership in bringing about such change. A model for facilitating, and for leading, mission congregations follows:

A framework for facilitators

This model is developed from the work of James Hopewell's seminal book, *Congregations*. In it, and particularly in chapter two, he reviews over two hundred books on the subject of congregational life and 'how to make your church grow'. He identifies four broad types which he calls *contextual, mechanistic, organic* and *symbolic*. The following diagram is built on his work. It incorporates spirituality at the heart of a church's nature, and uses (hopefully) more accessible terminology.

Spirituality is seen here as at the heart of a church's life. It is shaped by all four factors, as it also shapes a church's relationship to each element. A facilitating process would consist of enabling a church to allow all four elements to be in creative dialogue with the church's core values. In such

42

a dialogue both aspects would have the power to shape and evangelise each other. So, for example a church in cardboard city ought to have a spirituality significantly different from a church of the suburbs.

Setting points to the various studies which focus on the context of a church as decisive for it's own self-understanding and sense of mission. Typically this is expressed in the work of mission audits. This is a vital element. However, it is not sufficient of itself for it actually focuses on what is 'other than the church'. The phrase 'the church for others' has no meaning or existence unless it becomes a sentence: 'We are the church for others'. When that happens a creative dialogue can begin between the 'we' and the 'others'.

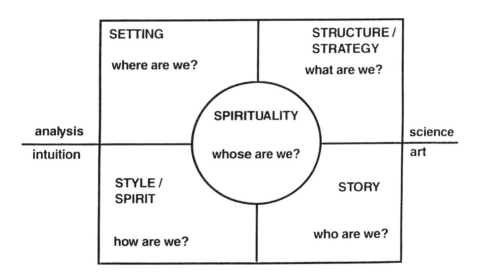

figure four: A framework for facilitators

Structure studies consider the vision, purpose, organisation and management of the local church. Typically church growth studies have focused the church's attention on this aspect of its make up. Structure plays the same role in the Body of Christ as the skeleton in the human form. It is essential framework, but certainly not the whole story. The lessons learned from industry and management have enabled the church to function and exercise leadership, more effectively. However, the church is more than an organisation, it is an organism. Which is why church

43

growth and management exercises on churches often do not produce the hoped for radical change thought to be available through better management. That will not happen unless such work is integrated into the total picture represented by the above diagram.

Style studies consider the church as a community. The church is seen as having a personality and being an organism with a life and character of its own. Community development studies and projects cover this aspect of the church's life. They point us to the fact that unless we have some understanding of the inner character and personality of a church we will achieve little working on its setting and structure.

Story studies are the primary focus of Hopewell's work and the one which he argues is both most neglected and most important. This includes the study of the history of a church and of its attitude to, and understanding of, itself through such reflection. He tells the story of one church which clearly, in the whole of its history, saw itself as the hero and approached every situation, especially in its missionary involvement with the surrounding community, in 'hero mode'. Once a church can see it is doing that, it gains the power to ask whether this is the truth of the situation and whether it is the most effective attitude to its work.

In the above diagram an axis has been drawn through the middle. Above the line are what can be consider the *analytical* work of understanding the church; this is the realm of *scientific* investigation of the church. This is where the church tends to focus its attention, not least because here it is looking at visible evidence. However, below the line are the hidden parts of the iceberg, namely the *intuitive* work of listening to and understanding the feel, atmosphere, and character of a church, and doing the *artistic* (literary) work of 'reading' the church's story. A good case can be made out for the church needing to put more work, thought and energy into understanding the 'below the line', hidden dynamics of the local church if fundamental change is to be brought about.

However the work of facilitation would seem to require not only enabling the full picture (all four corners of the church) to be seen, but for the spirituality to be shaped by, related to, and be allowed to evangelise, and be evangelised by, these four corners. What should emerge is a community with a conscious understanding of its story so far, of the character that has emerged out of that story, and of how – through encounter with God – the next chapter can be written as the church orders its life for its mission to the community of which it is part.

A framework for leaders

Whilst facilitators sit alongside the church and come from outside it, the leader and leadership sits within the church and functions to bring a new reality into being. Drawing on the work of facilitators, it is helpful to consider the following framework (see *figure five*, p.46) as providing a way of exercising leadership of a church making the pilgrimage into missionary being.

The large circle represents the world as the context for mission. This needs to be seen both as the global village, the whole created order to which God's redeeming purposes stretch, and also the more local city or community of which the church is a part. As such the church today often has to adjust to the fact that it, and its members, inhabit a number of worlds and communities, even if its parish boundaries suggest an over simple geographical framework.

> *The process of secularization has resulted in an amazing variety of interdependent worlds. Many people today live in a variety of worlds such as family, job, leisure, politics and education. These worlds represent different social structures.*
>
> The Church for Others, p.83

The norm of relating into today's work is within the framework of a sociological grid, which cuts across the traditional, rural, geographical grid. A missionary church will have its focus continually on this whole-life approach, weeping with those who weep, lamenting – as did Jesus – over those who see no need to weep, and rejoicing with those who rejoice. It is a church that sees the engagements of its members in the wholeness of human existence as the focus of its mission and the direction of its resources. It will worry more about, and work more for, the doctor or mother functioning in those roles, than about tasks they may have within the church.

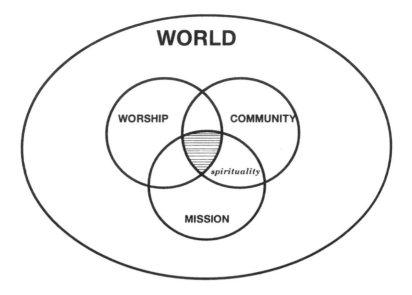

figure five: framework for leaders.

The *spirituality* appropriate to the setting, tradition (story), and present experience of the members needs to be such as is best designed to equip these people to live Christianly in this setting. Whilst needing to be enriched from many sources, such a spirituality also needs a sharpness of definition and character that makes it accessible to newcomers and practical enough to guide and enrich long-term participants in the church. It needs to be consciously considered, rather than unthinkingly handed down. It is a living and growing plant which needs both pruning and nurture, for it is the vine that holds the church 'in Christ' (John 15).

The *worship* of the church should be expressive of the church's spirituality, and of how that spirituality engages with the world around. It needs to see that its worship fulfils the two tasks of nourishing the spirituality of the members of the church, and – because worship is 'public worship' – communicating the spirituality of the church to those not yet part of the community of faith. As such the church needs to discover and develop rituals that relate. For example, the biblical practice of lamentation has immediate connection with a media-saturated culture. People come to church out of a world in which they are bombarded by the troubles of the global village. Expressing the pain and grief of the world is one way in which the church's worship can relate to the world around it. Another is the gift of hope in such situations, expressed and expounded through word, sacrament, and stories of hope.

The *community* dynamic of the church needs, like worship, to have the power both to express the spirituality of the church (so that how members relate gives concrete expression to the core values of the church), and also to be a door through which those coming, by personal friendship, within the ambit of the church may see beyond the individual friend to the community of faith. That community of faith needs to be sufficiently transparent for those coming into contact with the church to see the spiritual heart of the church and thereby themselves begin to encounter God. The church is community, not just an organisation. The mission of being 'fishers of men' is to be done not so much with line and hook, solitary work for those so inclined, but by laying down a network of loving relationship into which groups of people can feel they belong, find hospitality, and discover the presence of God. That is the work of a whole community.

The *mission* structures of the church need also to be shaped for the double dialogue between both the surrounding community (in obvious ways such as action with the homeless in areas where that is a major issue) and the spirituality of the church. Too easily the church has the mission structures (playgroups, pensioners lunches, etc), but has become cut off from its own core values. The mission structures then cease to be transparent to faith or engaged in mission. Too often the church has many bridges into the community, but the gospel seldom travels along such bridges.

There are two ways in which such structures need themselves to be evangelised. They need to be renewed in spiritual source. Forming a group which prays for the parents and children of the playgroup, for example, will almost invariably lead on to opportunities to care for, listen to and deal with major life issues. The other path of renewal lies in the development of new structures for mission. Parenting courses are one such new development taking place in the church at present. Others are emerging all the time. A missionary congregation will need to learn the costly art of letting go of inappropriate structures if it is to have the space and resources to develop fresh contemporary and appropriate models of mission for today's setting.

Towards a missionary priesthood

The task of leading a church to move into mission mode, involves helping it to reflect on all these aspects of its life and relationship to the world, with a view to making conscious choices about how it understands God's call to participate in his mission. Prayer, listening to one another, the surrounding setting and to God, resulting in courageous action in the light of that listening, are at the heart of such missionary leadership.

The shift to a mission mode of operating is unlikely to become reality without clergy finding help to discover a whole new way of seeing and living their role within the Christian community. What has already been said suggests a number of marks that the church will need to look for, and encourage to grow, in its clergy – and lay leaders.

The church needs leaders with vision who are also able to draw out the vision of others as well as to communicate their own. They will need to be like conductors of an orchestra, drawing out the gifts of the many and finding how best to harmonise them. They will need to be emotionally secure, and neither threatened by gifted, visionary and able, lay-people, nor lacking the ability to stand over against the congregation, when necessary. They will need to give theological help to lay people wrestling with the call of God to bear witness in the testing environment of many work situations. It is a vital and demanding task.

Canon Robin Greenwood, author of *Transforming Priesthood,* has helpfully identified the following five major developments which clergy need to engage with creatively and simultaneously. They are reproduced here in his words since they echo, from a different perspective, so much of what has been outlined above.

a)   a growing concern for discipleship

Increasingly laity recognise the importance of a developing spiritual journey which takes seriously their personal uniqueness.

b)   a holistic rationality

Taking into account feelings and particular contexts, as well as the intellect, there is a move among laity to want to understand the faith and to make connections with their occupation and the structures of society.

c)   a shared vision

In diocese, deanery and parish (and ecumenically) there is a move towards a shared mission statement and aims and objectives to make this a reality. This is related to the passionate concern of God for the wholeness of creation and is resourced not only from the past (the Scriptures, tradition, history etc) but also by a knowledge of God's final intentions for the unity of all things.

d) team learning

Instead of individuals in ministry, there is a profound move towards teams of all kinds of ministers, learning, worshipping and working in mutual strength and vulnerability. This is moving towards a church of rather than for people.

e) seeing the whole, being Catholic

Churches are moving towards seeing themselves as complex and open systems, engaging with the trinitarian God and the entire world. It is no longer regarded as appropriate either to remain separate from other parts of the local and world church or to blame others when things go wrong.

Concluding reflection

One way to look at what has been written above, is to consider the biblical themes that are likely to be most energising for the church's mission at the end of the second millennium. Four in particular stand out and are expressed in diagrammatic form below.

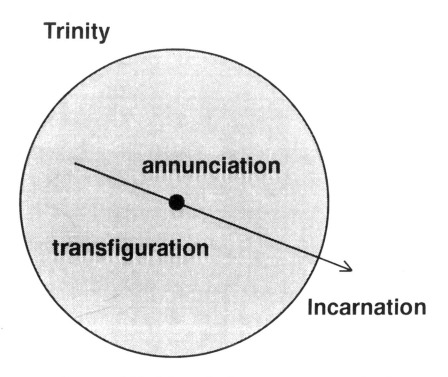

figure six: biblical themes for the emerging missionary church

The *Trinity* is foundational for the church's understanding both of the God who has revealed himself through Christ, and for the church's own self-understanding. The church has been invited into the hospitality of God (cf. Rublev's icon *The Hospitality of Abraham*), and as such stands within the circle of love defined by the two great commandments to love God and love others. The church is called, therefore, to be a network of loving relationship. If this circle of love is defined by the Trinity, it has its centre in encounter with God. Two incidents from the gospels express the nature of this encounter for today's church.

50

The *Annunciation*, in which the generative power of the Spirit broods over this new creation as in the first creation, points us to Mary as symbolic of the whole church. The church itself is the 'called out community' (*ecclesia* = called), addressed by God and called into such intimacy with the divine that Christ is formed in her (Galatians 4:19), as she listens to and responds to the words that God addresses to her. In worship the church encounters Christ afresh through word and sacrament; by the Spirit and in community, she is lead out through listening-obedience into life.

The *Transfiguration* points to the way in which the divine is intended to invade, energise, and transform (or 'transpose', as C.S. Lewis put it) the human. The foolish things speak wisdom to the wise, and the powerless discover authority to stand before the powers-that-be. Worship is one of the vital means through which the community of faith is transformed into the likeness of Christ (2 Corinthians 3:16-18). In the Eucharist the church is both formed through relationship to Christ, and transformed into his likeness. In this way it is equipped to go out and live the transformed life.

Christian mission is shaped by the *Incarnation,* the highest form of truth. Contrary to society's notion that abstract thought (as in 'pure' mathematics) is the highest form, the Christian faith points to lived-out-truth as containing more of the essence of the divine and the eternal, than the abstract (*orthopraxis* as the highest form of *orthodoxy*). It is this thrusting out into mission (the arrow in *figure six*) which expresses the apostolic ('sent') nature of the church.

Today's church would be well advised to return frequently to these themes for the enrichment of its vision, strengthening of its will, focusing of its vision, and shaping of its life and mission.

APPENDIX A

The marks of a missionary congregation

The following is a list of the marks of a missionary congregation. However, it is important to note that this is based largely on theoretical work. Another list needs urgently to be constructed out of observation of what actually happens on the ground. The two need then to be in dialogue. Either list has the potential to 'convert' the other list; both stand to gain and be enriched.

1. **Celebration.** This is taken in its widest sense and refers to the ability and desire to enjoy life and the gifts that God has given, and to participate in celebrating the new humanity modelled for us in Christ, opened up to humanity by his death and resurrection.

2. **Whole life Christianity.** Expressing faith in God in the whole of life. The focus of church life would shift from 'church organisations', to daily life – to the home, work place, and community life. The emphasis would be on personal growth, relational growth, and obedience to God 'in the market place' – with all its ambiguities. The church needs what has been called a 'hippopotamus spirituality – a spirituality suitable for surviving in the mud!'

3. **Simplicity.** Both in lifestyle ('enough is enough'), and in church structure. The institutional aspect will need to be significantly trimmed, as the church's life becomes outer-directed. Familiar landmarks will go. There will be no room for resources without vigorous pruning.

4. **Community.** Only a community living by a different set of values has the strength to witness prophetically to modern society. It cannot be done by lone rangers. Such 'community' involves building loving, honest relationships which stand out against the 'fragmented relatedness' of consumer culture.

5. **Empowering.** A missionary congregation is one that has broken out of the provider/client relationship into collaborative ministry and equipping individuals to make their contribution.

6. **Doing things differently.** The pastoral and maintenance church tends to be marked by doing different things (church groups and activities). A missionary church will be marked more by doing the ordinary things (work, leisure, family life) differently.

7. **Engaged.** A missionary church will be strongly engaged in the local community, and deliberately working with 'all people of good will' (see Raymond Fung, *The Isaiah Vision*).

8. **Distinctive.** Such a church multiplies the number of points of contact with the surrounding culture as its members live Christianly. This happens as effective initiation evangelises the whole person, including their world view, value system, personal identity, and lifestyle.

9. **Dimensional.** Enlightenment Christianity functions in separate compartments, spirituality and mission rarely connect. A missionary (and 'post-modern') congregation thinks of the depths of whole-life issues, and of the spiritual dimension within every issue.

10. **Still.** A missionary church will be an oasis of peace and quiet, in a frantic world, able not to be driven by doing but reflecting on experience before moving on.

APPENDIX B
For further reading

General

John Drane	*Evangelism for a New Age*	(Marshall Pickering, 1994)
James Hopewell	*Congregation*	(SCM, 1987)
Leonardo Boff	*Ecclesiogenesis*	(SCM)
Robert Warren	*Being Human, Being Church*	(HarperCollins, to be published May 1995)
WCC Report	*The Church for Others*	(WCC, 1968)

Culture

Graham Cray — *From Here to Where?* — Board of Mission Occasional Paper (Available from BOM, Church House, Great Smith St, London SW1P 3BN £1·95 incl. postage)

Diarmuid O'Murchu	*Our World in Transition*	(Temple House Books, 1992)
Bryan Appleyard	*Understanding the Present*	(Picador, 1992)
John Kavanaugh	*Still Following Christ in a Consumer Society*	(Orbis, 1991)
Lesslie Newbigin	*The Gospel in a Pluralist Society*	(SPCK, 1989)
	(and other books by Newbigin)	
Walter Brueggemann	*The Postmodern Imagination*	(SCM, 1978)
	(and other books by Brueggemann)	

Models

Derek Baldwin	*Open Doors Open Minds*	(Highland, 1994)
Raymond Fung	*The Isaiah Vision*	(WCC, 1992)
John A.T. Robinson,	*Liturgy Come to Life*	(Mowbrays, 1960)
Gary Smalley		
& John Trent	*The Blessing*	(Word, 1986)

Ordained ministry

Robin Greenwood	*Transforming Priesthood*	(SPCK, 1994)

Workbooks

John Cole	*How to be a Local Church*	(Kevin Mayhew, 1990)
John O'Shea	*Parish Project*	(HarperCollins, 1992)
Graham Cray	*Towards Tomorrow's Culture*	(CPAS, 1994)